DIVINE DISCOMFORT

Trusting God through the Pain, Tension and Unmet Expectations

Chase Qualls

Divine Discomfort: Trusting God Through Pain, Tension and Unmet Expectations

Copyright © 2025 Chase Qualls

All rights reserved. No part of this publication may be reproduced, distributed, or transmitted in any form or by any means, including photocopying, recording, or other electronic or mechanical methods, without the prior written permission of the publisher, except in the case of brief quotations embodied in critical reviews and certain other noncommercial uses permitted by copyright law.

Published by Vivid Virtue Publishing www.vividvirtuepublishing.com

Scripture quotations taken from the Holy Bible, New International Version® (NIV®). Copyright © 1973, 1978, 1984, 2011 by Biblica, Inc.™ Used by permission. All rights reserved worldwide.

Opening Scripture and Prayer:

Jeremiah 29:11

"For I know the plans I have for you," declares the Lord, "plans to prosper you and not to harm you, plans to give you hope and a future.

Prayer

Lord, give me the wisdom of discernment, the power to move at Your direction, ears to hear, eyes to see, and the will to do what You've called me to—especially when it's inconvenient. Bless the reader and the hearing of Your Word. Let this devotional minister to them and those around them. Let it provide peace, reassurance, and guidance that YOUR timing is... ALWAYS... on time.

Amen.

Divine Discomfort: Trusting God Through Pain, Tension and Unmet Expectation

Testimony and 30-Day Devotional Outline

By Chase Qualls

Acknowledgments

First—thank You, God—for loving me, Your mercy, favor, grace, and blessings.

To my Grandma Juanita ("Nita One") and Grandpa William Blue—your legacy of faith, prayer, and love still shapes our family. Grandma, I miss your laughter, your hugs, and hearing you call me "Bud." Grandpa, our time was brief but powerful—I carry those memories with deep gratitude.

Mom—thank you for your unwavering love and constant prayer. As a child battling asthma, you stayed up countless nights just listening to make sure I was breathing. As a single mother, you endured more than your share of challenges and inconveniences, yet you always made sure I felt encouraged, cared for, and deeply loved. Not a day goes by I don't recognize the blessing of being your son. I love you, Momma. You embody everything Grandma and Grandpa poured into you—and now into me

Aunties Leslie and Dorthea—thank you for your prayers, wisdom, and laughter. Being the oldest grandchild was a gift, especially with you guiding me.

To my cousins—I love cheering you on. To my brother and sister—though miles may separate us, our bond is unshakable. And to my brother in Christ, Frank—thank you for your testimony and encouragement.

And, to Kendra, Theodore, Seylah, Micah—BG and Jojo—I love you beyond words. You are my joy, my light, and a daily reminder of God's goodness.

Introduction

First, I didn't plan to write this devotional book.

It began with a friend's testimony-raw, real, and quietly profound. He had prayed, asking God to help him grow spiritually. Not long after, he was offered a new job. It paid well. It seemed like an answer. But there was a catch: it was an hour and a half away. Every day, he had to drive to the station to take the train.

In gratitude—and some frustration—he asked God, "Why would You bless me with a new job so far from home?"

I could hear Frank's initial confusion as he talked about the exhausting commute and the challenge of traveling such a long distance every day.

And that's when it hit him—those long train rides gave him something he never had before:

time.

Time to sit still.

Time to read the Word.

Time to pray and listen.

The very thing he first saw as a burden became the sacred space where God drew him closer.

Wow, I thought. What an incredible testimony—one that brought both revelation and blessing. I'm grateful I was there to witness it. His focus had shifted, and in sharing his story, it brought clarity. It reminded me that sometimes your testimony isn't just for you—it's also for the one listening.

That moment stuck with me. It stirred something deep and impactful.

How often do we assume that God's blessings should feel comfortable? That when He says "yes," it will come with ease?

But what if the answer is wrapped in discomfort—because that's what we really need? What if the delay, detour, or disruption... is part of the design?

This devotional with reflection questions, scriptures, and prayer, are for those moments.

Each day will guide you to examine your actions, realign your goals, and reaffirm your faith. Trusting that even in moments of pain, tension or unmet expectation, God is divinely doing something intentional. This is not about perfection-it's about presence. It's not about our convenience-it's about His calling.

May each day help you see more clearly: the truth may be inconvenient and uncomfortable, but it is never without purpose.

How to Use This Book

A Testimony, Reflection, and Devotional Journey

This book is designed to meet you in the tension—where prayers feel unanswered, your expectations unmet, and life just doesn't make sense. It's in this space that God often does His deepest work.

Part 1 contains five short chapter reflections rooted in testimony—real moments of spiritual tension, disruption, and growth. These are designed to prepare your heart for the 30-day devotional journey that follows. You can read them all up front or reflect on one per week.

Part 2 is a 30-day devotional experience. Each day includes:

- A Scripture to anchor your thoughts
- A personal reflection to challenge your expectations
- A prayer to realign your heart
- A journaling prompt for processing
- A daily action to walk it out

You're encouraged to move one day at a time, allowing the Lord to speak even in the pain and the quiet tension. The pace is yours, but the invitation is clear: trust Him—even here.

To get the most out of this journey:

- Set aside quiet time daily (even 10–15 minutes)
- Journal honestly—God can handle your questions
- Use the weekly themes and review days to track your spiritual growth

Whether you're in a season of waiting, grieving, stretching, or surrendering, Divine Discomfort is here to remind you: God is present in the pain, working in the tension, and faithful in the unknown.

Welcome to the journey into exploring His Divine Discomfort.

Contents

Acknowledgments	vii
Introduction	ix
How to Use This Book	xi
PART I: Testimony & Reflection	1
1. The Convenience Trap - When Our Faith Expects Easy	3
2. Divine Disruption	9
3. Sacred Inconvenience	13
4. Surrendering the Schedule	17
5. Inconvenient Transformation The Glory in the Detour	21
6. Conclusion: From Theory to Walk	25
PART II: 30 Day Devotional	29
30-Day Devotional Outline	30
Daily Prayer – Day Index	63
Daily Reflections (Insights) – Day Index	65
Daily Actions – Day Index	67
Scripture Reference – Day Index	71
About the Author	76

PART I
Testimony & Reflection

Chapter 1:
The Convenience Trap – When Our Faith Expects Easy

Recognizing Our Expectations

We may not say it out loud, but many of us enter our faith journey with a quiet assumption: *If I follow God, life should get easier.* Prayers will be answered quickly. Doors will open smoothly. Peace will be constant. Struggle, detours, and delay? Those must mean we did something wrong—or that God isn't paying attention.

This mindset is what I call **the convenience trap**: the belief that faith should be easy and fast, that favor should be frictionless, and that God's "yes" should always feel good. But both Scripture and life tell a very different story.

We often misinterpret promises like:

This verse from Matthew is often quoted in moments of stress, but it's also often misunderstood:

"Come to me, all you who are weary and burdened, and I will give you rest. Take my yoke upon you and learn from me, for I am gentle and humble in heart, and you will find rest for your souls. For my yoke is easy and my burden is light."— **Matthew 11:28–30 NIV**

It sounds like a promise of ease—but it's really a promise of **alignment**.

Jesus invites us to take His yoke, a farming tool that connects two animals to plow together. That means shared weight, direction, and submission. His "easy yoke" doesn't mean life without friction—it means we're walking in step with Him.

And that's the tension:
- We expect comfort, but God offers **companionship through difficulty**.
- We want release; He offers **refinement**.
- We long for convenience; He builds **character**.

"For no matter how many promises God has made, they are 'Yes' in Christ. And so through Him the 'Amen' is spoken by us to the glory of God." – **2 Corinthians 1:20 NIV**

We claim the "yes," but forget that the promise is fulfilled *through Him*, not by us—or on our timeline. That's a deeply challenging and inconvenient truth to accept.

The Comfort Expectation

Let's be honest—we're conditioned for comfort. Culture rewards speed, simplicity, and ease, built around convenience: one-click ordering, drive-thru fast food, instant messaging, and overnight shipping. So when it comes to God, we often apply the same lens, thinking something like this:

"God, if You love me, make this easy."

But God isn't a vending machine. He's

- **A Father**

    "This, then, is how you should pray: 'Our Father in heaven, hallowed be your name...'" — Matthew 6:9 NIV

    Jesus explicitly teaches His disciples to address God as Father—affirming His relational intimacy and loving authority.

- **A Refiner**

    "He will sit as a refiner and purifier of silver; he will purify the Levites and refine them like gold and silver." — Malachi 3:3 NIV

    A reminder that God is purifying us through fire—not punishing, but refining.

- **A Guide and Builder of Faith**

    "Fixing our eyes on Jesus, the pioneer and perfecter of faith..." — Hebrews 12:2 NIV

    He's both the Author and the Finisher of our faith. He starts it, strengthens it, and shapes it through every challenge we endure — maturing us.

The Disappointment That Follows

When reality doesn't match our expectations, disappointment creeps in with questions:

- "Why is this taking so long?"
- "Why didn't He stop the pain?"
- "Why would He answer like *that*?"
- "Why didn't He answer me at all?"
- "Why do I feel so alone?"

Unchecked, disappointment becomes disillusionment. We may retreat. Stop praying. Or silently (and sometimes openly) question God's goodness—not because He failed, but because our expectations were unrealistic or misplaced.

Biblical Examples – When God Didn't Make It Easy
Moses – Delayed but Not Denied

Moses spent 40 years in Midian after fleeing Egypt before God called him to lead:

> "When Pharaoh heard of this, he tried to kill Moses, but Moses fled... and went to live in Midian." – **Exodus 2:15 NIV**

> "After forty years had passed, an angel appeared to Moses in the flames of a burning bush." – **Acts 7:30 NIV**

Joseph – From Betrayal to Blessing

Joseph was sold by his brothers and unjustly imprisoned. Years later, he stepped into the very role God had prepared for him:

> "They pulled Joseph up out of the cistern and sold him..." – **Genesis 37:28 NIV**

> "Joseph's master took him and put him in prison..." – **Genesis 39:20 NIV**

> "I hereby put you in charge of the whole land of Egypt." – **Genesis 41:41 NIV**

Mary – Favored and Misunderstood

Mary was highly favored by God—but viewed with suspicion by the world:

> "Greetings, you who are highly favored! The Lord is with you." – **Luke 1:28–30 NIV**

> "She was found to be pregnant... Joseph had in mind to divorce her quietly." – **Matthew 1:18–19 NIV**

Jesus – Pain and Suffering for a Greater Purpose

Even Jesus—the Son of God—took the road of suffering to fulfill His mission:

> "My Father, if it is possible, may this cup be taken from me. Yet not as I will, but as You will." – **Matthew 26:39 NIV**

> "He was pierced for our transgressions... the punishment that brought us peace was on him." – **Isaiah 53:5 NIV**

> "He humbled himself by becoming obedient to death—even death on a cross!" – **Philippians 2:8 NIV**

That last verse? It's not meant to sound extreme—it *is* extreme. Jesus' sacrifice was excruciating, sorrowful, and devastatingly uncomfortable and painful. And yet it was the only way to secure our salvation.

Thank you, Jesus!

What God Really Promised

God never promised convenience—He promised **closeness**. He never guaranteed ease—He guaranteed **endurance**.

He didn't say the road would be smooth—He said He'd never leave us on it alone. And just so we don't mistake blessings for immunity:

"He causes his sun to rise on the evil and the good, and sends rain on the righteous and the unrighteous." – **Matthew 5:45 NIV**

What we often label as *inconvenient* may actually be *intentional*.

Let This Sink In

The trap of convenience says, "God, work on my timeline."

But faith says, "God, Your will be done—even when it's slower, harder, or unfamiliar."

Let this reflection loosen your grip on instant answers—and open your heart to deeper trust. Because sometimes what feels like delay is just the beginning of a better, more faithful story and testimony to share.

Reflection Questions

1. Where have I confused the expectation of comfort or unclear confirmation?
2. Have I confused delay with denial—especially when comfort was disrupted?
3. What expectations of God might need to be surrendered or changed?

Chapter 2:
Divine Disruption

When God's 'Yes' Looks Different

Introduction

We love the idea of answered prayer. But what happens when God says "yes"—and it feels like disruption?

We pray for growth and experience stretching.

We ask for strength and face struggle.

We seek clarity and find ourselves in a fog of confusion.

God's answers are real and definitive, but seldom convenient.

The Disruption Reality

Disruption is one of God's most misunderstood tools. We tend to see it as interference. He uses it for alignment.

We call it delay—He calls it development.

We see disappointment—He's setting direction.

"For my thoughts are not your thoughts, neither are your ways my ways," declares the Lord. – **Isaiah 55:8 NIV**

The longer we walk with God, the more we come to appreciate:

God's "yes" often feels like "no" at first—because it rarely comes the way we expect.

Disruption in Scripture

Abraham – A Yes That Required Relocation

God's promise to Abraham to make him into a great nation, and many blessings began with a massive life disruption:

"Go from your country, your people and your father's household to the land I will show you. I will make you into a great nation, and I will bless you.." – **Genesis 12:1-2 NIV**

No GPS. No roadmap. Just obedience.

Jonah – A Yes That Involved a Storm and a Fish

Jonah's call came with resistance—and correction:

"But the Lord provided a huge fish to swallow Jonah, and Jonah was in the belly of the fish three days and three nights." – **Jonah 1:17 NIV**

Sometimes God's "yes" shows up in the belly of what we tried to escape.

The Disciples – A Yes That Led Into a Storm

Jesus sent His disciples into a situation He knew would shake them:

"Immediately Jesus made the disciples get into the boat and go on ahead of him..." – **Matthew 14:22 NIV**

The storm wasn't a punishment. It was a platform for Peter's next level of faith.

Lazarus – A Yes That Looked Like a Tragedy

Jesus didn't rush to prevent Lazarus' death. He waited on purpose:

"So when he heard that Lazarus was sick, he stayed where he was two more days." – **John 11:6 NIV**

Resurrection reveals more glory than recovery ever could.

Disruption ≠ Disapproval

We tend to interpret resistance as rejection, but divine disruption isn't a sign that God is against us—it's often proof He's working on something bigger.

"Consider it pure joy, my brothers and sisters, whenever you face trials of many kinds, because you know that the testing of your faith produces perseverance." – **James 1:2–3 NIV**

God's path to growth rarely travels through convenience. It walks straight through surrender.

The Blessing Beneath the Breaking

Disruption uncovers what comfort conceals:

4. Our idols – We often elevate people, possessions, platforms, or our plans above God's will. Disruption shakes those pedestals—reminding us that **anything we're unwilling to surrender has become a spiritual idol**. Sometimes it's the job we prayed for, the relationship we thought would complete us, or the comfort we confused for calling. When broken, it hurts—but it also frees us.

5. Our pride – Comfort feeds the illusion of control. But when life turns upside down, we realize just how little control we have. Disruption humbles us—not to shame us, but to **open us to grace**, to a position of surrender that invites God to lead.

6. Our overreliance on self – We say "God is my source," but often live as if we're our own providers, planners, and protectors. Inconvenience exposes the fragility of that mindset, pushing us to lean into God's strength instead of striving in our own. **It's in weakness that His power is made perfect.**

7. Our shallow prayers – When everything's going well, our prayers can become routine or transactional. But in the valley of pain, we cry out more intently. We listen more closely. We pray differently. **Disruption revives intimacy with God**—and in doing so, transforms our prayer life from surface-level to soul-stirring.

God's "yes" can break us, but only to build something stronger.

"He cuts off every branch in me that bears no fruit... every branch that does bear fruit he prunes so that it will be even more fruitful." – **John 15:2 NIV**

Reflection Questions

8. Where has God's "yes" felt like disruption in your life?
9. What outcomes are you expecting that may need to be surrendered?
10. What might God be building through the very situation you're praying He removes?

_____
_____
_____
_____
_____
_____
_____
_____
_____
_____
_____
_____
_____
_____

Chapter 3
Sacred Inconvenience

The Purpose Behind the Delay

Introduction

Few spiritual experiences are more frustrating than waiting. We pray, we obey, we step out in faith—and then nothing changes. Or worse, things seem to get harder. In these moments, it's tempting to believe God is ignoring us, or that we've somehow missed His will.

But what if the delay isn't a detour? What if it's divine?

We often view delay as wasted time. But in God's hands, delay is **sacred ground**. A place of preparation. A space of transformation.

Delay Is Not Denial

Delay can show up in many forms. Delay in answering a prayer or delay in seeing something come as He has promised. God's silence does not mean absence. His delay isn't rejection.

More often, it's the preparation for a promise that requires maturity to carry.

"For the revelation awaits an appointed time... Though it linger, wait for it; it will certainly come and will not delay." – **Habakkuk 2:3 NIV**

What God Does in the Waiting

Waiting is not passive. It's where some of the deepest spiritual work happens. In seasons of silence, God:

11. Realigns our focus
12. Deepens our dependence
13. Breaks down pride
14. Builds up trust

Like a seed buried in the soil, the transformation begins long before anything is visible on the surface.

"But those who hope in the Lord will renew their strength. They will soar on wings like eagles…" – **Isaiah 40:31 NIV**

Biblical Proof That Delay Is Sacred

Jesus – Hidden Until the Appointed Time

Even Jesus, the Son of God, waited 30 years before beginning His fully public ministry.

"But when the set time had fully come, God sent his Son…" – **Galatians 4:4 NIV**

He was never late—just perfectly on time.

David – Anointed but Not Yet Crowned

David was chosen as king while still a teen, but spent years in hiding before stepping into the throne.

"So Samuel took the horn of oil and anointed him… from that day on the Spirit of the Lord came powerfully upon David." – **1 Samuel 16:13 NIV**

"David stayed in the wilderness strongholds and in the hills… day after day Saul searched for him." – **1 Samuel 23:14 NIV**

God used the wilderness to shape David into a king who could handle the weight of the crown.

Sarah – A Promise That Outlived Her Expectations
Sarah waited 25 years for the fulfillment of a promise she barely believed could still happen.

"Is anything too hard for the Lord? I will return to you at the appointed time next year, and Sarah will have a son." – Genesis 18:14 NIV

God's timeline honored His faithfulness, not our logic.

Job – Trusting When Nothing Makes Sense
Job's story reminds us that Divine Discomfort isn't always short-lived. He lost his wealth, health, and family—and endured not just pain, but silence from God.

"Though he slay me, yet will I hope in him; I will surely defend my ways to his face." – Job 13:15 NIV

Through seasons of suffering, Job held onto faith in a God he didn't fully understand. And when the testing was done, God restored more than Job had before.

Sometimes what feels like devastation is actually divine formation.

Delay Develops Dependence
Waiting reveals what we truly believe. Do we trust God for *who He is*, or just for *what we want from Him*?

"Be still before the Lord and wait patiently for him..." – Psalm 37:7 NIV

When we learn to wait well, we gain more than just the answer—we gain intimacy.

Reflection Questions
15. How do you typically respond when God delays?
16. Can you look back and see how a past delay led to greater development?
17. What might God be forming in you right now, even if you can't see it yet?

Chapter 4
Surrendering the Schedule

Learning to Trust Divine Timing

We love a well-timed plan. There's comfort in calendars, confidence in control, and peace in predictability. But God's timeline doesn't operate on our schedule—it operates on His sovereignty. And that can be incredibly inconvenient.

Have you ever heard the saying, *"If you want to make God laugh, tell Him your plans"*?

I'm grateful He has a great sense of humor, because we've shared many laughs together. I've experienced more than a few moments where I confidently handed God my plans... only to be lovingly reminded who's actually in control.

To walk with God means surrendering not just *what* happens but *when* it happens.

The Illusion of Control

We don't just want a breakthrough—we want it *by Friday*. We don't just want an answer— we want it to fit into our timeline.

But divine timing isn't meant to frustrate us—it's meant to **form** us.

"There is a time for everything, and a season for every activity under the heavens." – Ecclesiastes 3:1 NIV

Spiritual Disciplines That Build Trust in God's Timing

Letting go of the need to control timing doesn't come naturally. But God gives us practices that help us release the clock and cling to Christ.

1. Sabbath Rest – Stop Striving

"In repentance and rest is your salvation, in quietness and trust is your strength." – Isaiah 30:15 NIV

Rest is a declaration: *God is in control. I am not.*

2. Prayerful Release – Cast the Burden

"Cast all your anxiety on him because he cares for you." – 1 Peter 5:7 NIV

Prayer doesn't just change outcomes—it changes our *outlook*.

3. Scripture Meditation – Anchor in Truth

"Your word is a lamp for my feet, a light on my path." – Psalm 119:105 NIV

When you can't see what's ahead, meditate on what God has already said.

4. Journaling – Recognize the Hidden Progress

"Write down the revelation and make it plain..." – Habakkuk 2:2

Sometimes the biggest breakthroughs happen subtly and quietly. Writing becomes a way to trace God's hand—even when your heart feels overwhelmed or your eyes can't yet see what He's doing. Journaling helps you spot the fingerprints of God you might have otherwise missed.

Biblical Examples of Divine Timing Joseph
From Forgotten to Favored

Joseph interpreted dreams in prison—and was forgotten for two more years.

"The chief cupbearer, however, did not remember Joseph; he forgot him." – Genesis 40:23 NIV *"So Pharaoh sent for Joseph, and he was quickly brought from the dungeon."* – Genesis 41:14 NIV

When God moved, He did it suddenly. But the waiting was necessary for both the opportunity *and* the readiness.

Jesus – Miracles on God's Clock

Even Jesus honored divine timing. At the wedding in Cana, His mother urged Him to intervene. He replied:

"Woman, why do you involve me? My hour has not yet come." – John 2:4 NIV

Even miracles have appointments.

Living in Trust, Not Tension

God's timing stretches our faith. But it also shields us from premature promotion and prepares us for the promise.

"Trust in the Lord with all your heart and lean not on your own understanding; in all your ways submit to him, and he will make your paths straight." – Proverbs 3:5–6 NIV

Trusting God means letting go of artificial deadlines and resting in His divine design.

Reflection Questions

18. Where are you still clinging to your personal timeline?
19. Which spiritual discipline might help you surrender more deeply?
20. Can you look back and see a time when God's delay protected or prepared you?

Chapter 5
Inconvenient Transformation The Glory in the Detour

Transformation rarely happens when everything goes as planned. More often, it's born in the frustrating, uncomfortable, and uncomfortable moments that reroute our lives and reshape our hearts.

We think we need a breakthrough. God knows we need to be **rebuilt**.

We pray for the straight path—but God, in His mercy, leads us through **the detour**. And it's there, in the unexpected turns, that He does His deepest work.

The Detour Develops Us

What we call setbacks, God calls set-ups. The detour you didn't choose may be the exact path that produces the faith, humility, and character you were missing.

"And we know that in all things God works for the good of those who love him, who have been called according to his purpose." – Romans 8:28 NIV

We quote this verse often—but rarely do we admit how inconvenient that "good" often feels in the moment.

Biblical Detours That Led to Glory

Ruth – From Loss to Legacy

Ruth didn't plan to lose her husband or leave her homeland. But she clung to Naomi and followed God's prompting—right into her destiny.

> *"Where you go I will go, and where you stay I will stay..."* – Ruth 1:16 NIV

> *"So Boaz took Ruth and she became his wife... she gave birth to a son."* – Ruth 4:13 NIV

That detour from Moab to Bethlehem led her into the lineage of Jesus.

The Israelites – The Long Way Around

God didn't take Israel on the fastest route to the Promised Land—He took them on the one that would protect and prepare them.

> *"When Pharaoh let the people go, God did not lead them on the road through the Philistine country, though that was shorter. For God said, 'If they face war, they might change their minds and return to Egypt.'"* – Exodus 13:17 NIV

Sometimes God delays the route to preserve the promise.

Becoming in the Middle

We tend to fixate on arrival—God focuses on who we become on the way. We want completion—He also wants **transformation**.

> *"Being confident of this, that he who began a good work in you will carry it on to completion until the day of Christ Jesus."* – Philippians 1:6 NIV

The journey changes you. That's the point.

What God Forms in the Detour

21. **Humility** – because you're no longer steering
22. **Wisdom** – because you've been forced to wait

23. **Compassion** – because you've been wounded
24. **Endurance** – because you didn't quit
25. **Faith** – because you walked when you couldn't see

God is not just guiding you **to** something — He's building something **in** you.

Reflection Questions
26. What detour in your life challenged you — but ultimately changed you?
27. How have you seen God's hand in a route you didn't plan to take?
28. Are you willing to embrace transformation, even when it interrupts your preferences, why are why not?

_____
_____
_____
_____
_____
_____
_____
_____
_____
_____
_____
_____

Conclusion: From Theory to Walk

If there's one truth that echoes through every chapter of this book leading to the devotional, it's this:

God's way rarely aligns with our convenience our expectations — but it always aligns with our transformation.

We've explored how:

- Our expectations can trap us (Chapter 1)
- God's "yes" often disrupts more than it delivers — at first (Chapter 2)
- Delay isn't wasted time, it's sacred time (Chapter 3)
- Surrendering control opens us to deeper peace (Chapter 4)
- The detour is often the destination for our growth (Chapter 5)

Each story, example, and verse points back to one divine truth:

discomfort, pain, and tension isn't evidence of God's absence — it's the backdrop of His most intentional work.

Faith Is Meant to Be Lived

Reading truth is one thing. **Walking it** is another.

That's why the next section of this book invites you into 30 days of reflection, Scripture, and practical faith-building action. Not because you need more content—but because transformation requires **rhythm, honesty, and space**.

This devotional section isn't designed to give you perfect answers. It's meant to give you **anchored perspective** in those imperfect moments.

Each day, you'll receive:
- A Scripture grounded in truth
- A short reflection rooted in real life
- An insight to chew on
- A simple prayer
- A step to live it out

Let Pain and Tension Lead You Deeper

You may be entering this next chapter of your faith journey from a place of frustration, waiting, or surrender. Or maybe you're walking in peace—but want to stay grounded when the unexpected comes.

Either way, this devotional is your invitation to meet God in the middle of the mess—not after the miracle.

Take a deep breath.

Open your heart.

And trust that every moment is an invitation. Let's walk this out together—one day at a time.

RECAP:
TRUSTING HIS TIMING THROUGH OUR UNMET EXPECTATIONS

- God's timing is perfect, even when it doesn't match our own.

- Pain and discomfort can draw us closer to Him.

- Surrender your unmet expectations to God in prayer.

- God offers comfort and renewal to those who seek Him.

- Trust in His faithfulness, even when the outcome is unknown

PART II
30 Day Devotional

Divine Discomfort: Trusting God Through Pain, Tension and Unmet Expectations

30-Day Devotional Outline

Section 1: The Unexpected Yes (Days 1–6)
  - A Yes Wrapped in Distance
  - The Answer You Didn't Picture
  - God's Plans > Our Preferences
  - When Favor Feels Frustrating
  - You Prayed for Growth, Not Comfort
  - From the Ask to the Assignment

Section 2: Delayed, Not Denied (Days 7–12)
  - Waiting Is Not Wasting
  - Lazarus Was Still Loved
  - The Wilderness Prepares the Warrior
  - In the Meantime, God Is Moving
  - Trust the Slow Walk
  - God's Timing Builds Trust

Section 3: Obedience Before Outcome (Days 13–18)
- Noah Built Without Rain
- Abraham Left Without a Map
- Peter Stepped Before the Storm Ceased
- Joshua Walked in Circles
- Naaman Wasn't Healed Until He Dipped
- You Don't Need All the Details to Say Yes

Section 4: Faith in the Inconvenient (Days 19–24)
- Blessing in the Burden
- The Fire Was Necessary
- Paul's Chains Had Purpose
- The Road to Damascus Was Disruptive
- Jesus Took the Long Road to the Cross
- Comfort Can't Produce Calling

Section 5: From Inconvenience to Intimacy (Days 25–30)
- The Train Became a Tabernacle
- The Cave Became a Calling
- God Is Closer in the Climb
- Your Delay Is Someone Else's Delivery
- Reframing the Frustration
- The Inconvenient Path to Divine Purpose

Day 1

A Yes Wrapped in Distance

"For my thoughts are not your thoughts, neither are your ways my ways," declares the Lord.

ISAIAH 55:8

Reflection: The new job was a blessing—but it came with a long commute. In frustration, he questioned God's answer until he realized the time on the train allowed him to read, reflect, and grow spiritually.

Insight: God's yes may stretch us before it settles us.

Prayer: Lord, help me embrace the yes—even when it's uncomfortable.

Action: What current 'inconvenience' might actually be an answer to prayer?

_____

_____

_____

_____

Day 2

The Answer You Didn't Picture

"I am the Lord's servant," Mary answered. *"May your word to me be fulfilled."* Then the angel left her.

LUKE 1:38

Reflection: Mary's life was turned upside down by God's plan. His answer brought discomfort but also divine purpose.

Insight: God's answers are about purpose, not preference.

Prayer: God, help me say yes to what I don't understand.

Action: List two unexpected blessings in your life today.

_____

_____

_____

_____

_____

Day 3

God's Plans > Our Preferences

"Many are the plans in a person's heart, but it is the Lord's purpose that prevails."

PROVERBS 19:21

Reflection: Our plans offer comfort, but God's plans produce growth. Real transformation often begins with disruption.

Insight: God's plans will often override our comfort zones.

Prayer: Lord, let Your purpose prevail in my life.

Action: Surrender one personal plan to God's control today

_____

_____

_____

_____

_____

Day 4

When Favor Feels Frustrating

"The Lord was with Joseph so that he prospered, and he lived in the house of his Egyptian master."

GENESIS 39:2

Reflection: Joseph had favor—even in prison. Favor doesn't always mean freedom. Sometimes, it means preparation.

Insight: God's favor may come in uncomfortable packages.

Prayer: God, teach me to trust Your favor even when I feel confined.

Action: Reflect: where has God's favor felt frustrating or uncertain?

_____

_____

_____

_____

_____

Day 5

You Prayed for Growth, Not Comfort

> *"Consider it pure joy, my brothers and sisters, whenever you face trials of many kinds, because you know that the testing of your faith produces perseverance. Let perseverance finish its work so that you may be mature and complete, not lacking anything."*
>
> JAMES 1:2–4

Reflection: We grow through resistance, not ease. Challenges answer the prayer for deeper faith.

Insight: Growth never comes from comfort.

Prayer: Lord, strengthen me through discomfort.

Action: Write what discomfort is producing in you right now.

_____

_____

_____

Day 6

From the Ask to the Assignment

"So now, go. I am sending you to Pharaoh to bring my people the Israelites out of Egypt."

EXODUS 3:10

Reflection: Moses asked God to help his people, and God responded with an assignment. God's answers often come with a mission.

Insight: God's answers often come with assignments.

Prayer: Give me boldness to walk in what You've shown me.

Action: What's one step you've been avoiding after God spoke?

_____

_____

_____

_____

_____

_____

Day 7

Waiting Is Not Wasting

"Though it linger, wait for it; it will certainly come and will not delay."

HABAKKUK 2:3

Reflection: We often equate waiting with inactivity. But in God's timing, waiting is rarely idle—it's divinely intentional. When it feels like nothing is happening, God is refining, aligning, and preparing you for what's ahead. The waiting season is often where your roots grow deeper in faith.

Insight: God uses the "wait" to prepare you for the "weight" of the promise.

Prayer: Lord, help me wait with hope and not with doubt. Grow me in quiet places and give me faith to trust Your perfect timing.

Action: Write down one thing you're waiting on. Instead of asking why the delay, ask what are You developing in me through this?

_____

_____

_____

Day 8

Lazarus Was Still Loved

"So when he heard that Lazarus was sick, he stayed where he was two more days."

JOHN 11:6

Reflection: Jesus delayed going to Lazarus—not because He didn't care, but because His plan was bigger. Love sometimes waits, not out of neglect but to reveal greater glory.

Insight: God's delay is not His denial—it's often His design.

Prayer: Lord, help me remember that waiting doesn't mean forgotten.

Action: Think of a prayer you've waited long on. Trust that God's love is still active in the delay.

_____
_____
_____
_____
_____

Day 9

The Wilderness Prepares the Warrior

> *"The Lord who rescued me from the paw of the lion... will rescue me from the hand of this Philistine."*
>
> 1 SAMUEL 17:37

Reflection: Before David faced Goliath, he faced lions and bears—in secret. God uses private battles to prepare you for public victory.

Insight: Preparation often feels like isolation.

Prayer: God, help me see the wilderness as preparation, not punishment.

Action: Identify a hidden battle you've faced. What did it prepare you for?

_____

_____

_____

_____

Day 10

In the Meantime, God Is Moving

"And we know that in all things God works for the good…"

ROMANS 8:28

Reflection: Even when you see no movement, God is orchestrating your good. The meantime is not a vacuum—it's a workshop.

Insight: God is always working—even in your waiting.

Prayer: Lord, let me trust Your unseen hand.

Action: Write down three ways God could be working behind the scenes today

_____

_____

_____

_____

_____

Day 11

Trust the Slow Walk

"There is a time for everything…"

ECCLESIASTES 3:1

Reflection: We want microwave answers, but God often uses the crockpot. His process is slower—but far richer and deeper than we expect.

Insight: God's timing isn't rushed—it's refined.

Prayer: Give me patience, Lord, to walk in step with You.

Action: Where are you rushing ahead of God? Pause and realign today.

_____

_____

_____

_____

Day 12

God's Timing Builds Trust

"But those who wait on the Lord shall renew their strength…"

ISAIAH 40:31

Reflection: Waiting is not passive—it's an active dependence on God. It builds the kind of strength you'll need for what's ahead.

Insight: Waiting well is a sign of worship and trust.

Prayer: Help me worship while I wait, Lord.

Action: Take 5 minutes today to sit in silence and listen for God's voice.

_____
_____
_____
_____
_____

Day 13

Noah Built Without Rain

"By faith Noah... built an ark to save his family."

HEBREWS 11:7

Reflection: Obedience often looks strange. Noah obeyed God in faith, before there was any sign of rain. Faith acts before the evidence appears.

Insight: Obedience doesn't wait for confirmation—it walks by faith.

Prayer: Lord, let me follow even when I don't see results yet.

Action: What act of obedience is God calling you to today?

___

___

___

___

___

Day 14

Abraham Left Without a Map

"He obeyed and went, even though he did not know where he was going."

HEBREWS 11:8

Reflection: God didn't give Abraham the full blueprint—just the first step. Faith is not having all the answers, but following the One who does.

Insight: God gives light for the step, not the whole path.

Prayer: Teach me to move at Your word, even if the path is unclear.

Action: Take one obedient step today, even if the outcome is uncertain.

_____

_____

_____

_____

Day 15

Peter Stepped Before the Storm Ceased

"Then Peter got down out of the boat…"

MATTHEW 14:29

Reflection: Peter didn't wait for the waves to calm—he stepped out in the storm. Faith doesn't wait for ideal conditions. It steps at Jesus' word.

Insight: Faith shows up in the storm, not just the stillness.

Prayer: Give me boldness to walk toward You, even when the water is wild.

Action: What fear are you facing? Write it down. Step forward anyway.

_____
_____
_____
_____
_____

Day 16

Joshua Walked in Circles

"March around the city... once each day for six days."

JOSHUA 6:4

Reflection: Joshua obeyed God's strange instructions. Walking in circles felt pointless—but obedience broke the walls. Sometimes God asks for action that doesn't make sense—until it does.

Insight: Obedience may feel repetitive—but it's not wasted.

Prayer: God, help me trust Your instructions, even when they seem unusual.

Action: Is there something God's asked you to keep doing? Stay faithful today.

Day 17

Naaman Wasn't Healed Until He Dipped

"So he dipped himself... and his flesh was restored."

2 KINGS 5:14

Reflection: Naaman wanted healing his way—but God required humility. Breakthrough came after obedience, not before.

Insight: Sometimes healing waits on humility.

Prayer: Remove overconfidence and worldly pride, Lord, and lead me in humble obedience.

Action: Identify an area where you're resisting God's instructions—and surrender it.

_____

_____

_____

_____

_____

Day 18

You Don't Need All the Details to Say Yes

"Your word is a lamp to my feet..."

PSALM 119:105

Reflection: God often gives just enough light for the next step—not the full plan. Faith moves with what you've been given.

Insight: The details may come later—obedience is for now.

Prayer: Lord, give me peace with partial clarity and full obedience.

Action: What's one thing you've been waiting on more clarity to do? Take one step today.

Day 19

Blessing in the Burden

"But he said to me, "My grace is sufficient for you, for my power is made perfect in weakness. "Therefore I will boast all the more gladly about my weaknesses, so that Christ's power may rest on me."

2 CORINTHIANS 12:9

Reflection: Sometimes the burden you carry is the very thing God is using to build your dependence and deepen your faith.

Insight: The burden may be a bridge to deeper grace.

Prayer: Lord, help me trust that my weakness is a platform for Your power.

Action: Reflect on one burden you're carrying. What blessing might it be hiding?

_____

_____

_____

Day 20

The Fire Was Necessary

"He said, "Look! I see four men walking around in the fire, unbound and unharmed, and the fourth looks like a son of the gods."

DANIEL 3:25

Reflection: God didn't prevent the fire for Shadrach, Meshach, and Abednego—He joined them in it. Your fire may reveal His presence.

Insight: The fire you fear may be where your faith is forged.

Prayer: Help me not fear the flames, God, but look for You in them.

Action: Name a "fire" you're facing. Ask God to reveal Himself in it.

_____

_____

_____

_____

_____

_____

Day 21

Paul's Chains Had Purpose

"As a result, it has become clear throughout the whole palace guard and to everyone else that I am in chains for Christ."

PHILIPPIANS 1:13

Reflection: Paul's imprisonment advanced the Gospel. What looks like restriction might be God's redirection.

Insight: Your discomfort, pain or tension may be someone else's breakthrough.

Prayer: Lord, use even my limitations for Your glory.

Action: Think of how a testimony of setback in your life might serve others.

Day 22

The Road to Damascus Was Disruptive

"He fell to the ground and heard a voice say to him, "Saul, Saul, why do you persecute me?"

ACTS 9:4

Reflection: Paul's transformation came through divine interruption. Sometimes disruption is how God saves us from ourselves.

Insight: Disruption is often the doorway to destiny.

Prayer: Lord, disrupt what needs to change in me. Redirect me to Your purpose.

Action: Where has God interrupted your path? Write down the shift that followed.

_____
_____
_____
_____

Day 23

Jesus Took the Long Road to the Cross

"Father, if you are willing, take this cup from me; yet not my will, but yours be done."

LUKE 22:42

Reflection: Jesus chose obedience over ease. His path to victory was through suffering.

Insight: Redemption often walks a road paved with pain.

Prayer: God, help me choose obedience over ease, like Jesus did.

Action: Reflect on one area you've wanted to shortcut. Ask God for endurance.

Day 24

Comfort Can't Produce Calling

> "Then Jesus said to his disciples, "Whoever wants to be my disciple must deny themselves and take up their cross and follow me."
>
> MATTHEW 16:24

Reflection: The call to follow Jesus is a call to sacrifice. God calls us into something greater than comfort.

Insight: Calling costs something—but yields everything.

Prayer: Jesus, give me the courage to carry what You've called me to.

Action: Ask God what comfort you need to release to walk fully in your calling.

Day 25

The Train Became a Tabernacle

"He says, "Be still, and know that I am God; I will be exalted among the nations, I will be exalted in the earth."

PSALM 46:102

Reflection: That long commute became sacred space. Stillness in inconvenience creates intimacy with God.

Insight: Stillness invites divine intimacy.

Prayer: Lord, turn my delays into altars of encounter.

Action: Where can you carve out stillness today? Sit and seek God there.

Day 26

The Cave Became a Calling

> *"After the earthquake came a fire, but the Lord was not in the fire. And after the fire came a gentle whisper."*
>
> 1 KINGS 19:12

Reflection: Elijah's lowest moment came right before his next assignment. God meets us in the dark to prepare us for what's next.

Insight: God often speaks loudest in your loneliest spaces.

Prayer: God, help me listen when You whisper, even in my hiding.

Action: Spend 10 quiet minutes today asking God what He's calling you to next.

_____
_____
_____
_____
_____

Day 27

God Is Closer in the Climb

"I lift up my eyes to the mountains-where does my help come from? My help comes from the Lord, the Maker of heaven and earth."

PSALM 121:1–2

Reflection: Mountaintop moments are built through uphill battles. God meets you in the climb.

Insight: The climb sharpens your focus and builds your dependence.

Prayer: Lord, meet me in the struggle. Make me stronger through it.

Action: Think of your biggest challenge today. Invite God into it specifically.

Day 28

Your Delay Is Someone Else's Delivery

"Then the word of the Lord came to Jonah a second time:"

JONAH 3:12

Reflection: Your obedience impacts others. Jonah's delay affected a city—but God still used him.

Insight: Your obedience can unlock someone else's breakthrough.

Prayer: God, help me realize the ripple effect of my obedience.

Action: Reach out to someone today with a word of encouragement or action you've delayed.

___
___
___
___
___

Day 29

Reframing the Frustration

> *"Not only so, but we also glory in our sufferings, because we know that suffering produces perseverance; perseverance, character; and character, hope."*
>
> ROMANS 5:3–4

Reflection: Frustration may be the sign of formation. Let God grow you through what you didn't expect.

Insight: Frustration by discomfort can be God's tool for forming endurance and depth.

Prayer: God, change my perspective so I can see growth in the grind.

Action: List 3 things frustrating you today. Ask God what He's teaching you through them.

_____

_____

_____

_____

Day 30

The Inconvenient Path to Divine Purpose

"Do not conform to the pattern of this world, but be transformed by the renewing of your mind. Then you will be able to test and approve what God's will is-his good, pleasing and perfect will."

ROMANS 12:2

Reflection: Purpose often starts on paths we didn't plan. God's will rarely feels convenient— but it's always perfect.

Insight: Purpose is often on the other side of your preferences.

Prayer: Lord, I surrender my comfort for Your calling. Lead me fully.

Action: Pray over your next season. Ask God to realign your plans with His purpose.

_____

_____

_____

Daily Prayer – Day Index

Day 1: Lord, help me embrace the yes—even when it's uncomfortable.

Day 2: God, help me say yes to what I don't understand.

Day 3: Lord, let Your purpose prevail in my life.

Day 4: God, teach me to trust Your favor even when I feel confined.

Day 5: Lord, strengthen me through discomfort.

Day 6: Give me boldness to walk in what You've shown me.

Day 7: Lord, help me wait with hope and not with doubt. Grow me in the quiet places and give me faith to trust Your perfect timing.

Day 8: Lord, help me remember that waiting doesn't mean forgotten. Day 9: God, help me see the wilderness as preparation, not punishment. Day 10: Lord, let me trust Your unseen hand.

Day 11: Give me patience, Lord, to walk in step with You. Day 12: Help me worship while I wait, Lord.

Day 13: Lord, let me follow even when I don't see results yet.

Day 14: Teach me to move at Your word, even if the path is unclear.

Day 15: Give me boldness to walk toward You, even when the water is wild.

Day 16: God, help me trust Your instructions, even when they seem unusual.

Day 17: Strip me of pride, Lord, and lead me in humble obedience.

Day 18: Lord, give me peace with partial clarity and full obedience.

Day 19: Lord, help me trust that my weakness is a platform for Your power.

Day 20: Help me not fear the flames, God, but look for You in them.

Day 21: Lord, use even my limitations for Your glory.

Day 22: Lord, disrupt what needs to change in me. Redirect me to Your purpose.

Day 23: God, help me choose obedience over ease, like Jesus did.

Day 24: Jesus, give me the courage to carry what You've called me to.

Day 25: Lord, turn my delays into altars of encounter.

Day 26: God, help me listen when You whisper, even in my hiding.

Day 27: Lord, meet me in the struggle. Make me stronger through it.

Day 28: God, help me realize the ripple effect of my obedience.

Day 29: God, change my lens so I can see growth in the grind.

Day 30: Lord, I surrender my comfort for Your calling. Lead me fully.

Daily Reflections (Insights) – Day Index

Day 1: God's yes may stretch us before it settles us.

Day 2: God's answers are about purpose, not preference.

Day 3: God's plans override our comfort zones.

Day 4: God's favor may come in uncomfortable packages.

Day 5: Growth never comes from comfort.

Day 6: God's answers often come with assignments.

Day 7: God uses the wait to prepare you for the weight of the promise.

Day 8: God's delay is not His denial—it's often His design.

Day 9: Preparation often feels like isolation.

Day 10: God is always working—even in your waiting.

Day 11: God's timing isn't rushed—it's refined.

Day 12: Waiting well is a sign of worship and trust.

Day 13: Obedience doesn't wait for confirmation—it walks by faith.

Day 14: God gives light for the step, not the whole path.

Day 15: Faith shows up in the storm, not just the stillness.

Day 16: Obedience may feel repetitive—but it's not wasted.

Day 17: Sometimes healing waits on humility.

Day 18: The details may come later—obedience is for now.

Day 19: The burden may be a bridge to deeper grace.

Day 20: The fire you fear may be where your faith is forged.

Day 21: Your inconvenience may be someone else's breakthrough.

Day 22: Disruption is often the doorway to destiny.

Day 23: Redemption often walks a road paved with pain.

Day 24: Calling costs something—but yields everything.

Day 25: Stillness invites divine intimacy.

Day 26: God often speaks loudest in your loneliest spaces.

Day 27: The climb sharpens your focus and builds your dependence.

Day 28: Your obedience can unlock someone else's breakthrough.

Day 29: Frustration is God's tool for forming endurance and depth.

Day 30: Purpose is often on the other side of your preferences.

Daily Actions – Day Index

Day 1: What current 'inconvenience' might actually be an answer to prayer?

Day 2: List two unexpected blessings in your life today.

Day 3: Surrender one personal plan to God's control today.

Day 4: Reflect: where has God's favor felt frustrating?

Day 5: Write what discomfort is producing in you right now.

Day 6: What's one step you've been avoiding after God spoke?

Day 7: Write down one thing you're waiting on. Instead of asking why the delay, ask what are You developing in me through this?

Day 8: Think of a prayer you've waited long on. Trust that God's love is still active in the delay.

Day 9: Identify a hidden battle you've faced. What did it prepare you for?

Day 10: Write down three ways God could be working behind the scenes today.

Day 11: Where are you rushing ahead of God? Pause and realign today.

Day 12: Take 5 minutes today to sit in silence and listen for God's voice.

Day 13: What act of obedience is God calling you to today?

Day 14: Take one obedient step today, even if the outcome is uncertain.

Day 15: What fear are you facing? Write it down. Step forward anyway.

Day 16: Is there something God's asked you to keep doing? Stay faithful today.

Day 17: Identify an area where you're resisting God's instructions—and surrender it.

Day 18: What's one thing you've been waiting on more clarity to do? Take one step today.

Day 19: Reflect on one burden you're carrying. What blessing might it be hiding?

Day 20: Name a "fire" you're facing. Ask God to reveal Himself in it.

Day 21: Think of how a setback in your life might serve others today.

Day 22: Where has God interrupted your path? Write down the shift that followed.

Day 23: Reflect on one area you've wanted to shortcut. Ask God for endurance.

Day 24: Ask God what comfort you need to release to walk fully in your calling.

Day 25: Where can you carve out stillness today? Sit and seek God there.

Day 26: Spend 10 quiet minutes today asking God what He's calling you to next.

Day 27: Think of your biggest challenge today. Invite God into it specifically.

Day 28: Reach out to someone today with a word of encouragement or action you've delayed.

Day 29: List 3 things frustrating you today. Ask God what He's teaching you through them.

Day 30: Pray over your next season. Ask God to realign your plans with His purpose.

Scripture Reference – Day Index

Day 1: Isaiah 55:8 – "For my thoughts are not your thoughts, neither are your ways my ways," declares the Lord.

Day 2: Luke 1:38 – "I am the Lord's servant," Mary answered. "May your word to me be fulfilled." Then the angel left her.

Day 3: Proverbs 19:21 – "Many are the plans in a person's heart, but it is the Lord's purpose that prevails."

Day 4: Genesis 39:2 – "The Lord was with Joseph so that he prospered, and he lived in the house of his Egyptian master."

Day 5: James 1:2–4 –"Consider it pure joy, my brothers and sisters, whenever you face trials of many kinds, because you know that the testing of your faith produces perseverance.

Let perseverance finish its work so that you may be mature and complete, not lacking anything."

Day 6: Exodus 3:10 –"So now, go. I am sending you to Pharaoh to bring my people the Israelites out of Egypt."

Day 7: Habakkuk 2:3 – "Though it linger, wait for it; it will certainly come and will not delay."

Day 8: John 11:6 – "So when he heard that Lazarus was sick, he stayed where he was two more days."

Day 9: 1 Samuel 17:37 – "The Lord who rescued me from the paw of the lion… will rescue me from the hand of this Philistine."

Day 10: Romans 8:28 – "And we know that in all things God works for the good…"

Day 11: Ecclesiastes 3:1 – "There is a time for everything…"

Day 12: Isaiah 40:31 – "But those who wait on the Lord shall renew their strength…"

Day 13: Hebrews 11:7 – "By faith Noah… built an ark to save his family."

Day 14: Hebrews 11:8 – "He obeyed and went, even though he did not know where he was going."

Day 15: Matthew 14:29 – "Then Peter got down out of the boat…"

Day 16: Joshua 6:4 – "March around the city… once each day for six days."

Day 17: 2 Kings 5:14 – "So he dipped himself… and his flesh was restored."

Day 18: Psalm 119:105 – "Your word is a lamp to my feet…"

Day 19: 2 Corinthians 12:9 But he said to me, "My grace is sufficient for you, for my power is made perfect in weakness. "Therefore I will boast all the more gladly about my weaknesses, so that Christ's power may rest on me.

Day 20: Daniel 3:25 He said, "Look! I see four men walking around in the fire, unbound and unharmed, and the fourth looks like a son of the gods."

Day 21: Philippians 1:13 As a result, it has become clear throughout the whole palace guard and to everyone else that I am in chains for Christ.

Day 22: Acts 9:4 He fell to the ground and heard a voice say to him, "Saul, Saul, why do you persecute me?"

Day 23: Luke 22:42 "Father, if you are willing, take this cup from me; yet not my will, but yours be done."

Day 24: Matthew 16:24 Then Jesus said to his disciples, "Whoever wants to be my disciple must deny themselves and take up their cross and follow me."

Day 25: Psalm 46:10 He says, "Be still, and know that I am God; I will be exalted among the nations, I will be exalted in the earth."

Day 26: 1 Kings 19:12 After the earthquake came a fire, but the Lord was not in the fire. And after the fire came a gentle whisper.

Day 27: Psalm 121:1-2 I lift up my eyes to the mountains-where does my help come from? My help comes from the Lord, the Maker of heaven and earth.

Day 28: Jonah 3:1 Then the word of the Lord came to Jonah a second time:

Day 29: Romans 5:3-4 Not only so, but we also glory in our sufferings, because we know that suffering produces perseverance;

perseverance, character; and character, hope.

Day 30: Romans 12:2 Do not conform to the pattern of this world, but be transformed by the renewing of your mind.

Then you will be able to test and approve what God's will is-his good, pleasing and perfect will.

Closing Scripture and Prayer:
Deuteronomy 31:6

"Be strong and courageous. Do not be afraid or terrified because of them, for the Lord your God goes with you; He will never leave you nor forsake you."

Prayer

Lord, let us be thankful for this time of reflection in Your Word and for the many blessings You continue to pour out daily. You provide fresh mercy, grace, love, guidance, and wisdom—abundantly and faithfully.

Help us to lean into discomfort we often feel—whether it's waiting, facing delays, or feeling pain and tension. Thank You for reminding us that You are present even in those moments—especially when we don't yet understand or appreciate the answer.

Lord, grant us discernment and increasing wisdom to seek Your will—quietly, boldly, and consistently—even when it's inconvenient.

Thank You for Your steady hand, and for favor… in due season, for Your purpose, and for our good.

Amen.

About the Author

Chase Qualls is a seasoned sales leader, mentor, and man of faith who brings over 20 years of professional and personal experience to the page. Known for his authenticity, heart- centered leadership, and thoughtful communication, Chase is passionate about guiding others—whether in boardrooms, church halls, or everyday life.

As a husband, father, and committed member of his local church, Chase understands the tension between purpose and inconvenience. His insights into spiritual growth come not only from Scripture, but from his own walk through disruption, delay, and divine redirection.

Chase is the founder of Vivid Virtue Publishing, a platform dedicated to producing faith- inspired content that uplifts, equips, and speaks truth—especially when it's inconvenient. The Inconvenient Truth is his first devotional book, born out of prayer, personal testimony, and a desire to help others see God's purpose in life's interruptions.

He currently lives in Southern California with his wife and their children. When he's not writing or leading, you'll find him mentoring young adults, serving in ministry, or laughing with his family.

To connect with Chase,

visit: www.vividvirtuepublishing.com

Divine Discomfort: Trusting God Through Pain, Tension and Unmet Expectations

© 2025 Chase Qualls - All rights reserved.

www.ingramcontent.com/pod-product-compliance
Lightning Source LLC
Chambersburg PA
CBHW071956070426
42453CB00008BA/901